The Sun

The
Solar
System

The **Solar** System

Contents

©2016
Book Life
King's Lynn
Norfolk PE30 4LS

ISBN: 978-1-910512-83-8

Written by:
Gemma McMullen
Edited by:
Harriet Brundle
Designed by:
Matt Rumbelow
Ian McMullen

A catalogue record for this book
is available from the British Library.

Words in **bold** can be found in the glossary on page 24.

The Solar System

The Solar System is the Sun and
all of the objects that **orbit**, or go
around, it. Eight planets orbit the
Sun, including our home, Earth.

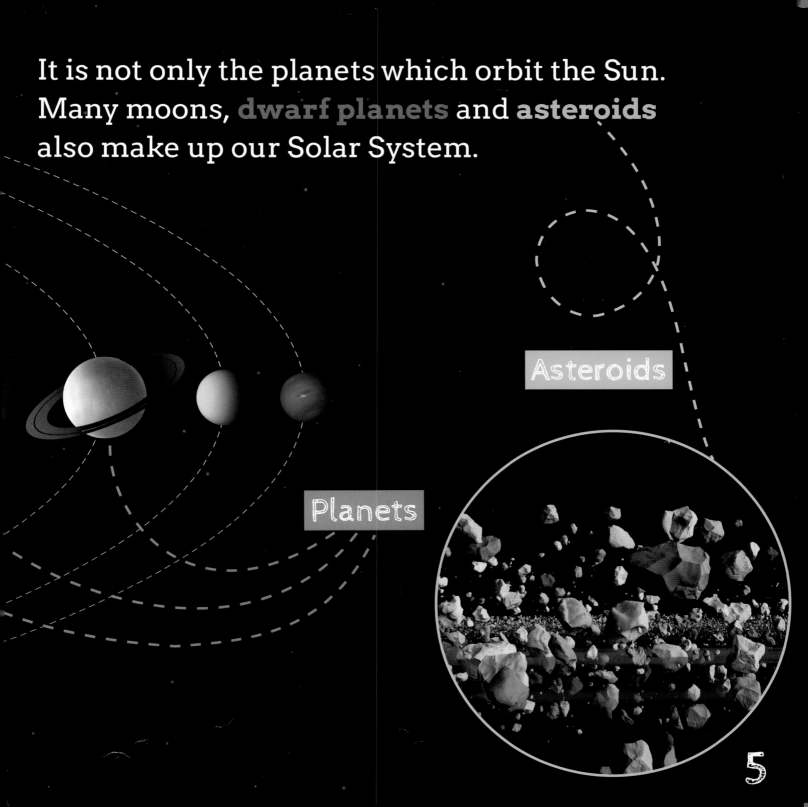

It is not only the planets which orbit the Sun. Many moons, **dwarf planets** and **asteroids** also make up our Solar System.

Asteroids

Planets

What is the Sun?

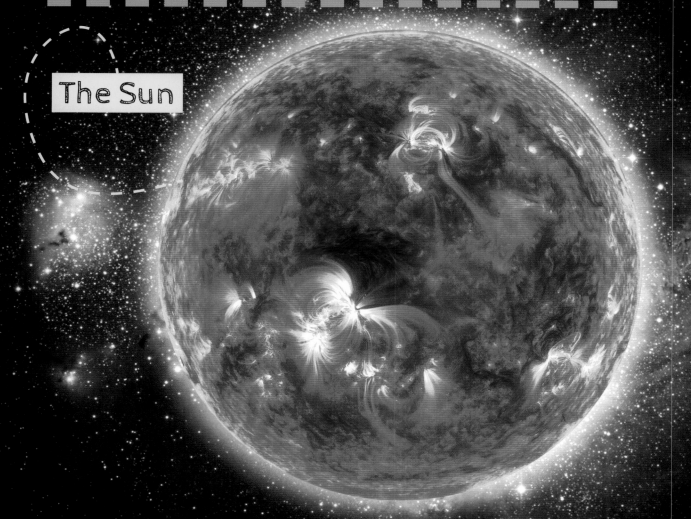

The Sun

The Sun is a star. Stars are giant balls of gas which are very hot and bright. The Sun is a yellow star. The centre of the Sun is its hottest point.

Some parts of the Sun are not as hot as the rest.
These parts are called sun spots.

Sun Spots

Creating Life

The Sun lights and heats the planets, including Planet Earth. All living things need the Sun.

Without the sun, Earth would be dark and cold. Plants could not grow so animals would have no food.

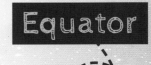

The middle of Earth gets the most sunlight. It is called the **Equator** and is the hottest part of the planet.

Where does the Sun go at Night Time?

Takes one day

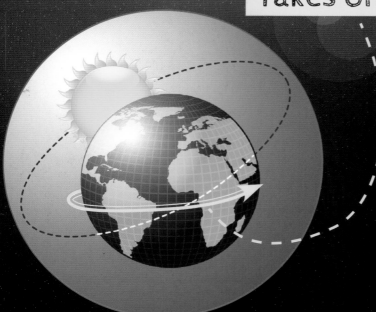

As well as going around the Sun, Earth is always spinning. It takes 24 hours (one day) for the Earth to turn around completely.

We cannot see the Sun at night because Earth has spun around. The Sun is lighting the other side of the globe.

11

The Moon

The Sun

Earth

The Moon

The Moon orbits Earth, as well
as the Sun. It is much smaller
than the Sun but looks a similar
size in the sky because it is much
closer to Earth than the Sun is.

The Moon has no light of its
own. It is bright in the sky
because the Sun lights it.

Solar Eclipse

Sometimes the Moon moves in front of the Sun. This is called a solar eclipse. As the sun's light and heat is being blocked, Earth becomes cold and dark for a short time.

The Moon

The Earth

The Sun

Looking directly at a solar eclipse can damage your eyes.

During a solar eclipse, animals get ready to go to sleep because they think that night time is coming.

15

Powerful Sun

The Sun is very powerful. Its strong rays can burn our skin. It is important to protect ourselves from the Sun with clothing and lotion.

Looking directly at the Sun could damage your eyes.

It is best to stay in the shade during the hottest part of a summer's day.

17

Which Planets are Closest to the Sun?

There are eight planets in our Solar System. All of the planets orbit the Sun. Mercury is the closest planet to the Sun. Its surface is very hot.

Earth is the third closest planet to the Sun. The planets which are furthest away are called Uranus and Neptune.

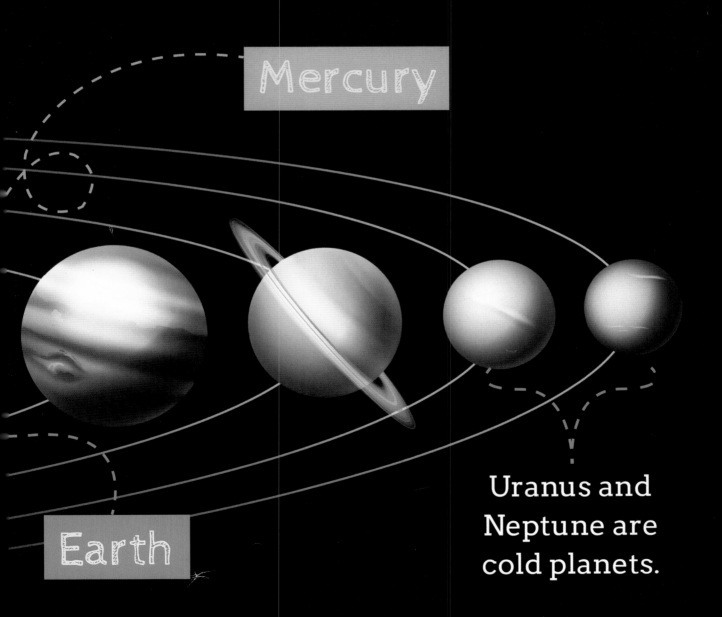

Mercury

Earth

Uranus and Neptune are cold planets.

The Other Stars

There are many other stars that we can see in the sky. They look smaller than the Sun but that is because they are further away.

A group of stars is called a galaxy.

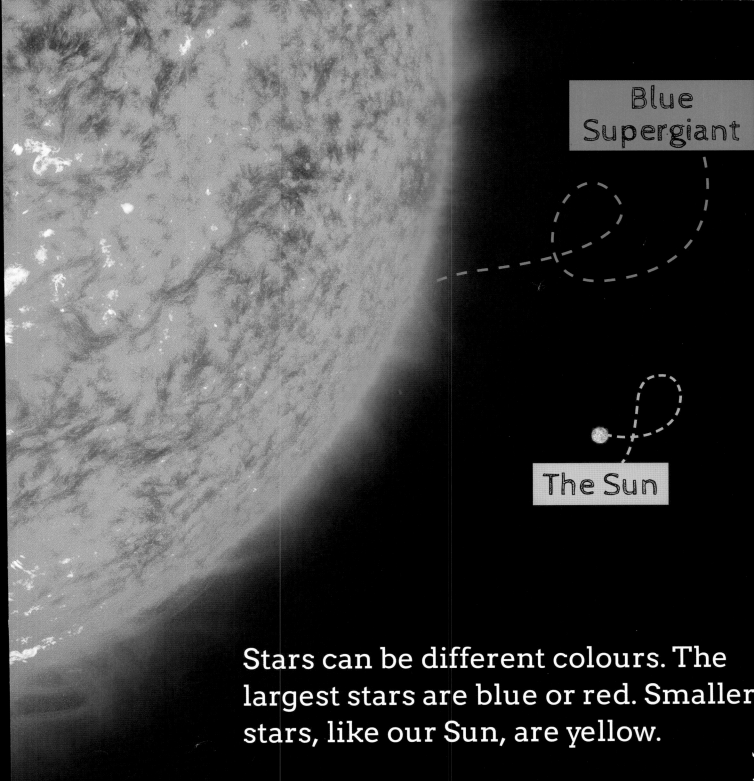

Blue
Supergiant

The Sun

Stars can be different colours. The
largest stars are blue or red. Smaller
stars, like our Sun, are yellow.

Super Sun!

1 It takes about 8 minutes for the Sun's light to reach Earth.

8 minutes

2 The Romans called the Sun 'sol'. In Ancient Greece the Sun was called 'Helios'.

3 The Sun is only *one* of *millions* of stars in the galaxy.

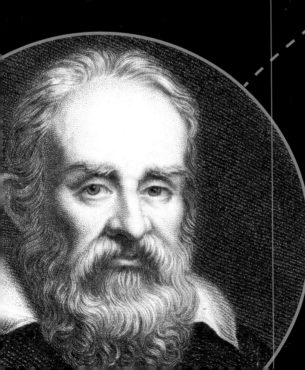

4 In the past, people believed that the Sun orbited the Earth, rather than the other way around.